"Ed helped me with the purchase of a new builder home. We were faced with many obstacles. Throughout the whole time, Ed maintained a positive attitude and made sure I closed on time no matter how many hurdles we had to get through."

– Priscilla G.

"Edward and his assistant, Jorge, were professional, organized, thorough and, most of all, kind and pleasant to work with. Thank you for being patient with me during my first buying experience and for protecting my financial interest."

– Nicola W.

"Ed was referred to us due to our purchasing circumstances (buying a home out of a trust). He is very professional, honest and fun to work with. It made the process easier and not such a burden. One thing I appreciated was he asked for everything upfront before we actually met (online application, financial statements, etc.). This cut down the need for follow-up items, dramatically making everyone's life easier. Ed was always there to answer questions (phone, text, email). Jorge, his junior loan officer, was also very helpful in all aspects. Thank you."

– Andy

"I am a first-time homebuyer and my broker recommended me to use Ed Fontes. When you are a first- time homebuyer, you are bombarded with loads of sparkling marketing when people are selling you their loan services, and it is so hard to chose the right, genuine service. You can't go wrong with Ed. I highly recommend him, because Ed keeps it real. He will tell you the facts and explain why you are getting what you are getting and helps ensure that your house will close on time with no hiccups. Ed and his fantastic team are on top of it and will help you get your loan approved at a great rate and with the quickest speed. I was able to get a lower rate and was able to close escrow within a month thanks to the efficiency and speed of Ed and his team. Highly recommended."

– Kimmy K.

"A GREAT experience working with Ed and his team. The loan process was smooth, no issues, and everything was explained in detail. The communication between him and his team and us were excellent. I am a first-time home buyer and had no idea what I was doing. Ed answered all of my ten-million questions quickly. I will be and have recommended Ed and hist team! Thank you for helping us find our home Ed!!"

– Kimberly R.

"Ed Fontes is a SUPER great loan consultant. Ed made the dreams come true for my buyer. My buyer desperately needed the loan right away because the first lender turned down my buyer's loan at the last minute. Ed finished the entire loan process in a short time. That was a miracle! Thank you very much, Ed. I will certainly recommend Ed to my clients for loans. Much appreciate your professionalism and the job well done."

– Kris F, agent

"I have met many loan officers throughout my career, and I must say without any doubt, Ed KNOWS his job. He knows that to get the job done, you must be willing to look at all options without any doubt. His willingness to get the loan for his client and the patience he conveys is absolutely admirable."

– Carlotta D, Broker

Ed is a well-known name in Sacramento lending, and he is a veteran mortgage broker. Ed combines an easy style and approachability with solid market mastery derived from years of service in the lending industry. I closed one of my transactions with Ed on a VERY difficult property. He got the deal closed, and I was impressed with his patience and dedication with a very difficult client. I highly recommend Ed to anyone looking for personal service combined with professionalism and unbeatable industry knowledge. He really knows his stuff, and his style is fun and warm."

– Alexander G, Broker

"Back in 2009, Ed helped make my dream of owning a house come true. I had been a single mom for a long time, and it was a struggle to get into a position where I could buy a home for my daughter and myself. Ed made that happen through his relentless efforts in ensuring all the bases were covered. Since then, Ed has helped me with refinancing to get me through the remodel of my home. I highly recommend doing business with this professional. He has an overwhelming knowledge base, and he is a great person to boot!"

– Jennefer C, U.S. Army Soldier

"Thank you, Ed for stepping up and helping the buyers on my listing! It's unfortunate the buyer's lender was a flake. We are all fortunate you step up and saved the day!" Thank You so much!"

– Estella D Real-Estate Broker

The Ultimate Guide to Finding the Perfect Home Loan
Copyright 2019 By Ed Fontes
All Rights Reserved.

All rights reserved. No part of this publication may be used or reproduced by any means, electronic, mechanical, graphic, including photocopying, recording, taping or by any information storage retrieval system or otherwise be copied for public or private use – other than "fair use" as brief quotations within articles and reviews – without prior written permission of the copyright owner.

ISBN: 978-1096331-73-5

The Ultimate Guide to Finding the Perfect Home Loan

7 Ways to Acquire Your Mortgage Without Stress and Overwhelm

ED FONTES

Dedication

I dedicate this book and lift it up to the Lord our God. With him all things are possible. To my wife, Maria, my backbone and partner in life of thirty-eight years as of this writing. Through thick or thin, the ups and downs, she has been by my side, helping in any way she can. I Love You Honey. To my children, Vanessa and Eddie. For always believing in me. For being the perfect children, a father would want to have. I thank God for bringing them into our lives.

To ALL who have helped me throughout my career who believed in me and my abilities to help them and their clients achieve the American Dream of home ownership! To Family and relatives, all my clients, past and present real-estate agents, loan officers and lending companies I have been affiliated with in the past and present as well as fellow associates.

Thank you!

Table of Contents

Introduction xi

Benefits of Owning a Home 1

There is a Loan for Everyone 17

Credit 27

Income-Qualifying 33

Assets 39

Collateral 43

Clear To Close! Who-Hoo! 47

Dreams Will Not Work Unless You Do

Introduction

For those of you that all you want in life is to achieve the American Dream of home ownership and the benefits that come with it.

"Never, never, never, never give up." –*Winston Churchill.*

Your dream will come true! This book was written to help you get there!

My goal writing this book is to hopefully help provide a better understanding of acquiring a home loan.

The seven ways are actually areas and explanations that will help lead you on the right path to becoming pre-approved for a home loan and what to expect, and thus owning your own home! But first let's talk about why you should own a home….

7 Ways to Achieve the Perfect Home Loan
Benefits of Owning a Home
There is a Loan For Everyone; Not All Loans are Created Equal
Credit
Income-employment
Assets
Collateral
Clear to Close

"Whether you think you can, or you think you can't—you're right."

-Henry Ford

Benefits of Owning a Home

There are a lot of reasons that someone wants to own a home:

1. Homeownership is a Form of Forced Savings

Paying your mortgage each month allows you to build equity in your home that you can tap into later in life for renovations, to pay off high-interest credit-card debt, or even send a child to college. As a renter, you guarantee that your landlord is the person who benefits from that equity.

2. Homeownership Provides Tax Savings

One way to save on taxes is to own your own home. You may be able to deduct your mortgage interest, property taxes, and profits from selling your home. But make sure to always check with your accountant first to find out which tax advantages apply to you in your area.

3. Homeownership Allows You to Lock in Your Monthly Housing Cost

When you purchase your home with a fixed-rate mortgage, you lock in your monthly housing cost for the next 5, 15, or 30 years. Interest rates have hovered around 4.5% since spring of 2018. In winter of 2018, rates increased to almost 6%. First-time home-buyer programs increased to 5.875% on a 30-year fixed. The value of your home will continue to rise with inflation, but your monthly costs will not. Regardless of rates, you can always refinance if rates drop. This has been accomplished by thousands of clients throughout the years.

4. Buying a Home Is Cheaper Than Renting

The results of the latest Rent vs. Buy report from Trulia show that homeownership remains cheaper than renting, with a traditional 30-year fixed rate mortgage in 98 of the 100 largest metro areas in the United States and 26.3% nationwide.

5. No Other Investment Lets You Live Inside of It

You can choose to invest your money in gold or the stock market, but you will need somewhere to live. In a home that you own, you can wake up every morning knowing that your investment is gaining value while providing you a safe place to live.

This should come before you go into the details First of all, you need to figure out your **"WHY"**. Why do you want to own a home? Is it because you are tired of paying rent? When paying rent, you are paying someone else's mortgage to a home you cannot make it your own. Is it because your whole family has always owned a home or homes? Is it because your friends own homes? Is it because you want the "write off" each home provides for the property taxes and mortgage interest? Is it because of just wanting to "Achieve the American Dream of Home Ownership"?

This last reason is the **"WHY"** for a lot of Americans, immigrants and residential aliens. It is pride. It is the feeling of your own dwelling in this country that you and you alone can own! This is America!

America that provides this freedom of owning your own home. The ability to create a home with your visions of a place to relax and call your own.

As you can see there are many benefits to owning a home. The first and foremost benefit is a lot of people enjoy the "write off" of owning a home. Besides having a place to call your own. Mortgage Interest and property taxes are the two that affect your income taxes tremendously. I must state here that I am not a tax expert. I always recommend consulting your tax expert in order to determine if this is a benefit for you. I can say that for all my clients throughout my career have experienced this benefit.

Other benefits are; the fact that the home is yours to do whatever you want with it! You can paint the colors of your choice. Remodel. tear out walls. Insert walls. Add a bathroom. Enlarge a kitchen. Create an environment that fits you inside and out. Add a pool and spa. Create an outdoor kitchen. Build a fire pit

One of my clients had children. When they purchased their home, there was a big oak tree in the front yard. They put a tire hanging from the tree for their children. They had a bench for them to sit while the children enjoyed swinging on that tire. I had other clients put a complete swing set in the front yard. Why? Because they had a small lot with a pool and cement in the backyard with no room for a swing set. All the kids in the neighborhood would come and play together. Do you find that odd? They didn't. it seemed perfectly normal for them to enjoy this benefit.

Another couple purchased a home because it had a six-car huge garage. They had a boat, motorcycles that needed to be garaged.

Another family of seven wanted a gourmet kitchen that fit everyone while they enjoyed cooking together.

Others wanted to be in a certain school district.

Many had to purchase in a different area and commute to work because of affordability.

A young couple purchased a duplex. They rented out one unit and lived in the other. This helped in paying their Mortgage payment.

As you can see, there are many benefits of owning your own home. Just figure your **"WHY"**. Write a list of all you desire, then narrow it down to specifics. This is the start.

Figure out first what it is that will fit your needs. The size of the home. The number of bedrooms, location and school district that will work best for you. Also remember this, when a family purchases a home into a neighborhood, they help increase the value of that neighborhood.

Let me explain; there is a lot of pride of ownership, excitement, enthusiasm when you purchase a home. You will create your own environment. Landscape, improve the appearance. Paint to protect the exterior and provide curb appeal that this home is yours. In other words, you help improve the neighborhood as well as the home itself. Many of my past clients did exactly this.

A year and a half later of home ownership, one of my clients came back for a refinance loan to eliminate the mortgage insurance. They had a little over $150,000.00 in equity! They were really excited! There was no way they could have saved that amount of money in a year and a half on their own! Truly one of the better benefits of owning a home. I want to caution you here. This does not happen all the time. There are some areas that will not achieve this amount of equity in that short period of time. Then there are other areas that even exceed this amount of equity. What you need to know is when you purchase a home, your mindset needs to be long term.

So, remember to write down a list of all the features of a home that you would like, and qualify them as follows:

'Must-Haves' – if this property does not have these items, then it shouldn't be considered. (as stated above, distance from work or family, school district, number bedrooms/bathrooms)

'Should-Haves' – if the property hits all of the 'must-haves' and some of the 'should-haves', it stays in contention, but does not need to have all of the features.

'Wish-List' – if we find a property in our budget that has all of the 'must-haves', most of the 'should-haves', and ANY of these, it's a WINNER!

Owning a home is not a get rich quick scheme. You are providing yourself a place called home for you and your family. Or future family. Think and find out what is your **"WHY?"**

How to Get Started Finding the Right Home Loan for Your Situation
Or The Do's and Don'ts of Finding a Lender

Let's look at the steps necessary to put you in a position to become pre-approved, ready to write your offer on that perfect home you've dreamed about . Ready to close your transaction within 10 days! Yes, that is right! By becoming pre-approved, doing all the work upfront will allow the opportunity for your offer to get accepted above all the others. Imagine a seller receiving two, three, four offers or more, and your offer is the only one that will close faster, providing the seller with money in hand, ready to move on!

Majority of the time, when our clients write an offer to close in ten days, we end up waiting for the seller. The delay usually ends up eleven to fifteen days to closing, which is okay because your offer was accepted!

Don't go with the flow! Find a lender who will be able to close your loan in ten days!

If not, then move on to another lender! This is the only way our offers become accepted! Sellers want their money fast. Especially if a home has been on the market for a long time! Doesn't that make sense?

As I write this book, 30-40% of my business is still turned downs from banks and other lenders that could not close client loans!

Yes. In today's economy and with social media, and the electronic and technology age, it still boils down to doing the work of processing a buyer's home loan properly to avoid being turned down. On those types of loans, we don't do bad loans, we do tough loans that fit the minimum guidelines. Besides, nobody wants to be turned down, right?

If you do not fit in the box with one of those so-called "ON-LINE" companies, you will not get a home loan through them. No matter how good you look on paper, there will always be a way to be turned down. Throughout my years, I've worked with many clients who have been turned down for a loan, yet we had no problem closing with the documentation provided to satisfy the minimum guidelines.

I have also learned how to avoid any issues that could arise during the process in order to be approved at the end of the contract and proceed to closing fast!

This is accomplished by doing everything upfront as well as, having the right attitude and teamwork with the other professionals involved; both listing agents and selling agents, coordinated inspections, and appraisals with sellers and buyers all coming together for a fast closing.

Before you go out and look at any homes, you must be ready to provide ALL documentation to become underwritten and pre-approved for the maximum you qualify for.

Do Not Go Out And Look At Any Homes Until You Know The Maximum You Qualify For! Until You Are Pre-Approved By An Underwriter!

You must have the "can-do" attitude to be ready to provide whatever is requested of you! This helps to expedite the process and close fast!

Once that is completed, your loan can close in as quickly as ten days! And don't you think a seller will be willing to take your offer above everyone's else because he will have a check in hand sooner than if he took one of the other offers? So, get to it!

I have never seen the perfect loan! Sure, a client may have a high FICO credit score, have the ability to put over 20% down or more of the purchase price, and have a great income, however, he or she may not have consistent income. Or, the client may have a great FICO scores, but change companies several times in the last two years. Or, someone just started his or her own business and does not have a full two-year history, but has low FICO credit scores, great income and low ratios. There are several reasons that could make or break the ability to qualify for a home loan.

Rest assured, I am here to enlighten you on the basics that you need to know to help you achieve the American Dream of home ownership!

You may be asked to provide more information, but realize that it is never a sign of your home loan going sideways, just that there may be other documentation needed to satisfy an underwriter's concern on your ability to afford the monthly payment of that home.

I have had several clients referred to me from other real-estate professionals. Some of those clients took two weeks, a month, or even two months to get approved. Real-estate agents would ask, "Why does it take so long to get pre-approved?"

Some of the issues are verifying your current and past employers if you do not have a complete two-year history as opposed to someone working for the same company for over two years or more.

One client's past employer took almost a month before getting us the verification of employment.

The real-estate agent who referred them to us was getting upset as to why was it taking so long. The clients were getting upset because we had to call them every time we could not reach their past employer's human-resource person. We were always given the run around that "so-and-so may be able to help you". Only to find out so-and- so did not have the authority to sign the form. So, it was difficult and time-consuming trying to reach the right person who could completely fill out the form.

Once we had formal approval, we closed the buyer's home loan within ten days. Was it worth the wait? You bet! They were able to acquire their home above everyone else's offer because of stating they would close fast! Everyone was extremely happy!

So, take the time to provide everything upfront including phone numbers, current and prior addresses and whatever your lender requests in order to help expedite your approval. Now bear in mind, there is a difference between a pre-qual and a pre-approval.

A pre-approval means your home loan is fully underwritten by an underwriter. Your home loan would be pre-approved for the maximum you could qualify for based on your income, assets and the loan program that best fits your needs.

What does a pre-qual mean then? A pre-qual means someone looked over your paperwork, ran an automated approval and said you are good to go. This means nothing on the paper it was written because none of your information has been verified. Thus the reason we see turn downs when you finally find a property and write an offer.

In my years in this industry there are two things that always occur:

1. The first one is when you are approved and ready to purchase your home, a professional realtor will find a home that really meets your needs, however, you are hesitant to write that offer. Why? Because you want to see what else is out there, right? That's just human nature.

I have seen and heard of this occurring quite often. Then after seeing five other homes, you decide you do like the first home that was shown to you, however, by the time you come around, it has already SOLD or has multiple offers! Urrgghh! Don't let this happen to you!!

If you like a home, write the offer, BUY IT! It is better to have your offer accepted and later change your mind than to want a specific property and not get it.

Your real-estate agent is a true professional who has done their homework on your exact needs. Listen to them.

2. The second thing is, sometimes, clients find a home and while going through the approval process of ordering the appraisal and title and escrow paperwork they start shopping for furniture or the new car to go with the new home.

DON'T purchase anything until you receive your keys to your new home! And DON'T have anyone check your credit!

I can recall several times, after repeatedly telling clients to not do anything, not even have someone check their credit while in the process, they have gone out and purchased items and said, "Oh we forgot. We were just so excited when our offer was accepted". **Don't be those people!**

One of our clients, first-time home buyers, a young couple, had signed their loan documents. The loan was getting ready to fund and close within a couple of days. Prior to the funding the loan there is always a back-door credit check to ensure that no new debt has been acquired. Well, they had gone out after the signing and purchased $5,000.00 in furniture on credit! They did not qualify for the home loan with the new credit debt! His father had to gift them the $5,000.00 to pay off the debt to close the transaction.

Again, do nothing, no credit inquiries, no new credit, no purchases of anything until your transaction is completed and you are handed the keys.

There will also be family members, friends, relatives and co-workers that will want to get involved in your business of purchasing a home and acquiring a home loan. Be courteous and be nice to them when they tell you your "rate is too high." "They have a friend in the business that has a lower rate." Or, you are "paying a lot of fees"**.**

All of a sudden, everyone seems to know our business and are the experts.

Unless your family members are experts in the lending and real-estate fields, it is best to listen to the professionals. When you are referred to a true, professional loan officer who has been in this industry for a long time, has a great reputation, and is all over the social- media sites providing education and information, then you can listen to them! It is because the professional realtor wants to ensure you will be able to qualify once your loan is approved without any hiccups, and your home loan will close smoothly! And that's what you want, isn't it?

In my years of experience, I have seen clients told by their parents, "Oh, go see so-and-so because your rate is too high". "So-and-so has this rate."(Sometimes, when a loan rate sounds to be true, it's because it is.) There are many times that parents, friends and relatives steer their kids wrong because they don't know that the going rates have increased and the economy has become stronger and there is a fear of inflation is on the horizon.

I usually tell my clients to call those companies their parents or friends refer them to. Some have decided to move their loans to another company, only to find out at the last minute that they could not get that rate, or it was an adjustable mortgage fixed for five or seven years, **BUT** it was amortized over thirty years, as they said… (Shysters will usually state it's a thirty-year loan, even though it is only fixed for five or seven years.) So, be aware.

I have had clients stay with me and were glad they did. I've had clients come back thirty days after they realized it was too good to be true. Some of those clients, unfortunately, wasted their time trying to save maybe forty dollars a month on the lower rate. And then, when they came back to me it turned out rates had increased, and they were stuck with the higher payment.

So, it is not always best to try and save pennies when in the long run you're spending lots of dollars.

Listen to the professional you were referred to.

Sometimes, parents, friends or family members could be out of touch with how our programs and contracts work nowadays. Times have changed, and so have the guidelines. In these cases, I ask, "When was the last time your parents or friends did a real estate transaction?" I have also asked, "Are your parents or friends moving in with you?" Again, when you are working with true professionals who have a solid reputation, you are ahead of the ball game.

One of my past clients were purchasing a new home and once we had them approved, we were waiting for the new home to be completed. During that time, a co-worker heard about them purchasing a new home. The co-worker referred them to a lender they had worked with. (Some lenders do not have experience in dealing with new-home communities, as is the case with this one lender). My clients ended up switching with them, even though I warned that they were not providing the true exact payment, which included additional taxes, called "mello-roos" and mortgage insurance, along with enough impounds for property taxes and insurance.

Sure enough, four months later, when the home was completed and the builder requested the loan to close, their lender ended up charging the clients extra fees and collecting more impounds for taxes and insurance, plus their payment increased almost four-hundred dollars!!! And the builder was charging $250 daily if they did not close on the contract date! OUCH!

So, they called me at that point. Unfortunately, I could not close their transaction within a couple of days as the contract mandated. It would have taken me maybe ten days or less.

In essence, the buyers' monthly payment increased over four-hundred dollars a month, along with having to provide additional funds at closing because they were dealing with an inexperienced lender doing a new-home-builder loan.

Again, when you are referred to a professional loan officer from a builder or a true real-estate professional, it is for this very reason. I even tell clients to google my name, so they know who they are dealing with. Don't be shy, Google your loan officer's name. Google the company name. And check out the reviews and testimonials!

We also work with many seasoned, experienced real- estate agents who we recommend you work with.

There are many loan programs out there that are geared to fit many clients' needs. Just remember, the higher the risk on the loan the higher the rate. We have had self-employed clients who could not acquire a regular home loan. However, because of their high deposits into their business accounts, we could use their business banks statements for the last twelve months to save and close on a home.. Of course, they had excellent credit and high FICO scores. Did they acquire a higher interest rate than normal? Yes, however, they could afford the payments.

Don't allow the rate to hinder you from purchasing a home loan. What goes up must come down as we have seen time and time again in our industry throughout the years. My first interest rate on my house was a 16% adjustable rate mortgage (arm) that could adjust to 21% the next month. We were tickled pink when we refinanced at 13.5%, then again at 9.5%. It's all relative because we sold that home with a lot of equity. Equity we would never have had to move up into our larger home had we not taken the original loan. Plus, we got the advantage of the tax write off for property taxes and mortgage interest.

I am not a tax expert nor portray myself to be one. The write off you receive depends on your own tax situation and I suggest you take that up with your tax accountant or CPA. I have thousands of stories and experiences with clients that could help you understand the process. Believe me, you will never be disappointed purchasing a home! Go for it!

"Just Do It!"

-Nike

There is a Loan for Everyone

There is a loan for everyone, but it's not necessarily the rate that should determine your loan choice. So, let me ask you something, are you rate driven? If so, why? Is it so you can brag about the rate you acquired to friends or relatives? If so, it's time to change your thinking. First, you need to know how much you can qualify for. That is what will give you the ability to close the loan! And, if you can't close the rate won't matter!

It is not always about the rate! It is about the ability to close the loan.

I have had clients who were so stubborn; they wanted a certain rate and they were willing to pay thousands of dollars in discount points to get it. And the only difference it made was maybe $50.00 less on the payment. A few years later, rates dropped. They came back to refinance. The thousands of dollars they paid went down the drain. Was it worth buying down the rate? Not in this case. But for them it was good because I must say that they did receive a write off for buying down the rate by paying discount points on their federal tax returns.

Discount points mean you are discounting the rate for a premium price/cost. When dealing with the majority of lenders or brokers, there are normally no points on the origination charge. An origination charge is usually for a processing fee and underwriting fee. I have had clients who shopped me, went to another lender on a rate that was advertised, then came back because they did not fit in the box for that lender to get that rate. But, by the time they came back, rates had increased.

It's not always about the rate.

I would also like to point out that you can acquire any rate you want if you are willing to pay for it, like in the example above. Remember that. By buying down the rate, that might be the only way for you to qualify for what you really want.

The standard lending programs are;

1. FHA (Federal Housing Administration) overseen by HUD (Housing of Urban Development)
2. VA Loans back by the Veterans Administration
3. Rehab loans
4. Conventional loans (backed by Freddie Mac and Fannie Mae)
5. Construction
6. Bank-statement loans (12 and 24 months)
7. First-time homebuyer programs. First Time Home Buyer programs have higher interest rates and fees. Majority of those programs are state driven. Some are bond programs or grants. Their rates and fees are non-negotiable.

As of this writing, we are seeing a lot of sellers willing to pay a portion of the buyers closing costs. It never hurts to have your real-estate agent request that for you. The only thing a seller can say is no, right? Think about it. If you are a seller and your house has not had any offers, would you do something to help get it sold? Offering to pay a portion of buyer's closing cost will help as we have seen time and time again! So, do not hesitate to ask.

Did you know that Interest rates are derived from the mortgage-backed securities (MBS) on the stock market? MBS is a safe haven for investors and their money in the stock market. It does not receive a huge return, but it does receive a steady return. Money flows into bonds, not only from people pulling money out of stocks, but from around the world. They give investors the ability to move money from one country to another whether the capital is sovereign or not. There are so many reasons why money would stay parked at the relative low return of bonds. This is why rates have nothing to do solely with stocks at all. There is still a lot of fear money plugged into bonds – especially U.S. Bonds.

So, with that said, did you know rates are affected by what occurs in our world? For example, when Greece and Italy both had their issues, interest rates dropped. Why? Because when investors saw this loss coming, they took their money out of their countries and invested them in MBS's in the United States as a safe haven, so they would not take drastic losses on their money.

In turn, we have a huge supply of money from those investors into the MBS. When that occurs, rates drop as they did during that time frame. The same is true when the market rallies. Investors take their money out of our MBS's and insert them into corporations or countries' corporations. Thus, the supply decrease, and rates increase because there is very little money available.

Or, there is fear of inflation from the FEDs. As you have seen, they will increase the rates to slow the market down. Therefore, everyone needs to know that interest rates will vary on a daily basis as the stock market does.

If you are quoted today, it may not be the same rate tomorrow or next week.

This is why it is important to get with a lender you are referred to. Get the process started, so you are in a position to lock in your loan. Recent clients had decided to gamble, to hold off on locking their loan. I do not gamble with my client's money. However, I subscribe to a service that alerts me when rates are starting to tank, or increase, as any top professional would. And I will call my clients and let them know rates are on the rise as I did with one of my clients. Not only did rates increase, they never came back down when it was time to close their purchase. They ended up with a payment $137.00 more than when they started! They gambled and listened to people who had no clue on rates.

Where did they acquire their information from? A crystal ball? I would like to know myself… No one controls rates!

So, when you are getting pre-approved, ask about locking your rate.

What is a rate lock, you ask? It is an arrangement between a lender and borrower to lock your loan for a certain period of time, 60-, 45-, 30-, or 15- day time frames. When you lock your loan, you usually get the current interest rates. Some lenders will choose to lock your rate immediately, just in case it increases. If rates increase, it could deter the amount you qualify for to a lower loan amount. A rate lock is an agreement, and it's important that both parties are bound by that agreement.

So, it really would depend on your lock period of where you want your rate to be. I know myself and other prominent lenders will share and show you where exactly the rates are at the time you are looking for a loan and the cost of locking.

Unless a change occurs to the loan application, the interest rate locked, will stay the same and not be affected by any market changes. When you lock your rate, there are advantages and disadvantages depending on where the market is.

An example would be that if all of the sudden the rates dropped drastically, the buyer would not be able to unlock his loan and acquire that lower rate. The same would be true for a lender if rates increased, they would not be able to increase the borrower's rate. As you can see, locking your loan shows a commitment on both the lender and the borrower to move forward together.

Rates are derived from many factors. I laugh when I am asked, "What is your rate?". That is a loaded question! If you are given a rate over the phone without knowing your situation, run! No one can tell you what the rate is until they have a complete picture of what the applicant credit picture is, the income (ratios), the amount of down payment, the loan amount, type of loan and type of property. If they really want an answer, I usually tell them a ballpark. I also let them know they are not doing justice to themselves because the difference between a 4.5% 30-year fixed rate and a 4.375% 30-year fixed could be only $20.00 – $40.00. And if they do apply for a home loan, rates could be higher.

As I mentioned, rates fluctuate on a daily basis governed by the law of supply and demand in the stock market of mortgage-backed securities. No one has any control when rates will increase or decrease.

The best thing to do is to complete a loan application and get into a position that you can lock your loan when you find your home.

FHA, VA, conventional, first-time homebuyer programs, jumbo, non-QM loans, bank-statement loans, expanded loans, investment loans, hard-money loans, construction loans, rehab loans.

Believe it or not, this statement of name of this chapter is so true in many ways. Yes, there are many loan types that can get you into a home. Do we see many people utilizing the various loan programs available? Yes and no.

The YES is because, sometimes, self-employed people have a lot of write-offs on their businesses and cannot qualify for a standard home loan. However, they qualify for the payments. Regular W2-employed individuals usually will acquire the standard FHA or conventional loan types unless you are a veteran, then you would acquire a VA loan (Veteran Administration loan) if you qualify.

If your loan exceeds the county limits, then you will be in a jumbo-loan category. These can become more stringent for qualifying. If you find a home that does not meet the standard qualifications of habitability, along with health and safety issues, then you will want a rehab loan.

Remember, there are loan limits for government and conventional loans in every county and state. I have included the websites that you can check to see where your loan limit is in your state and county;
    https://www.fha.com/lending_limits
    http://www.loanlimits.org/va/
    https://www.fanniemae.com/singlefamily/loan-limits .

In the Fannie Mae website, click on the left side where it states "Loan Limit Look-Up Table 2019". (or whatever the year is when you check) This will take you to search/scroll for your state and county limit.

FHA loans require a minimum of a 3.5% down payment. Conventional loans require a minimum of 3% if you qualify. The majority of loans require a down payment of 5% or more.

Anytime you are putting less than 20% down, you will be required to have mortgage Insurance (MI) on your conventional loan. FHA loans require mortgage insurance premium (MIP). These are amounts added to your monthly payment. They are included in the qualification and payment of your home loan.

Mortgage insurance protects the lender in the event you default on the loan. On a VA loan there is no monthly mortgage insurance. The VA loan includes a funding fee that is added to the loan amount. If you are a disabled veteran, this fee will be waived. If you are in the reserves or active duty, this funding fee will be reduced. Another great benefit for our veterans!

VA LOANS are, to this day, the true 100% financing. This is to say thanks to all our veterans. If you are a veteran reading this book, thank you for your service! I have also served in the Army. I know how these loans work. You will be required to provide your DD214 and complete the VA form 26-1880. Your lender will usually provide this to help expedite the process of acquiring your certificate of eligibility. If they do not know this form, then you need to go to a lender who does.

With the different scenarios to qualify for a home loan. You may not fit in the regular FHA, VA and conventional- loan box. If that's the case, then we would look at expanded programs. These programs would go off 12- to 24-month bank statements. They usually require a higher down payment of 20% or more, depending on the FICO scores of the borrower. Sometimes, we have seen borrowers put down as little as 10% due to their exceptional credit and funds available. These types of loans also have higher rates; they are fixed for a five-year or seven-year period, then they adjust monthly, every six months or yearly, depending on the program you acquire. Not everyone will take these loans.

It is always best to complete an application and have your file be pre-approved with an actual underwriter's disposition. Make sure you ask if this is how the lender operates. You want to make sure your home loan is underwritten with your income and asset documentation. By doing this, you will have already explored the type of loan that best suits your needs. Acquire your pre-approval! Then you are off house hunting!

A year ago today you wished you shoulda-coulda-woulda

One year from now you'll wish you had started today

Credit

In the old days, they used to call qualifying for a home loan by the three C's; credit – capacity – collateral. However, they have added one more to call it the four C's – capital (cash reserves).

Credit: Your history of paying bills and other debts on time.

Capacity: Your current and future ability to make your payments.

Collateral: The home, or type of home, that you would like to purchase qualifies as much as the buyer.

Capital: The money, savings and investments you have that can be sold quickly for cash.

Your credit is the most important factor in acquiring a home loan. Your credit score will determine your interest rate and program, depending on your down payment. When I hear clients tell me that so-and-so acquired a certain rate, and they want that rate, I usually state it will depend on their credit and credit scores, plus all the other factors that involve approving a home loan.

The majority of all lenders will use scores from 580 to 850. In all my years in this industry, I have never seen an 850. The highest was an 835. That score belonged to a grandmother that had over

$300,000.00 in credit cards with zero balances. She had several rental properties that were paid, free and clear. She wanted to refinance one of the homes for her granddaughter to attend Stanford University, an expensive private institution in California. How awesome was that? Chances are, most will not fit this scenario. Credit scores from 580 to 620 will usually put you into an FHA loan. There are very few lenders that will lend on a conventional- rate program within this credit-score range. If they do, they may require a higher down payment and higher rate. Rates will vary on your credit scores. The categories for rate changes are as follows; 580-620, 620-640, 640-680, 680-700, 700-720, 720-760. Anything above 760 acquires the best rates. Those rates are the ones you will see advertised. The majority of people are referred to me because they did not fit in that category with a lender advertising low rates.

Again, it's not always about the rate, but the ability to close your loan!

The majority of first-time homebuyer programs require a minimum credit score of 640. Other grant programs require a minimum over 660 or better. **The rates on first- time homebuyer programs will always be higher than the standard average rates publicized on regular home loans.**

There is no secret to your credit. Either it is good, or it is bad. I believe high schools in America should teach their students about fiscal responsibility: how to open and work a checking account; how to budget; how to save; and how to know that if you receive a 20% discount at a department store to open an account. (Without paying the bill in full, you will be paying double for the product or item from the interest derived from that purchase.) You cannot blame yourself for something you were never taught about.

Each loan program will decide whether to pay off collections or not. As of this writing, any lender would not require to payoff a medical "charge off" or "medical- collection account". These accounts should never be touched. If you pay off one of those accounts, it could jeopardize your FICO scores causing it to drop!

Yes, I have seen them drop when a client comes to me from another lender. The lender told them to pay off their collection accounts. That's a no-no if you want your scores to increase. Fico scores go back four years on their system. If you pay off the collections today, this is considered a new derogatory remark on your credit file. The four years will start all over again on the collection. Thus, the possibility of your score dropping.

There are many companies that offer to look at your FICO scores. Credit Karma is one of them. Unless you pay for an actual mortgage FICO-score credit, it will not be the same score when your lender will acquire your Mortgage Report. There are several score systems. One for credit cards and one for auto loans, and the one that encompasses all of them, which is the Mortgage Credit Report. There are many myths about running your credit and lowering your scores. They are all false unless you are repeatedly having someone running a hard check on your credit report several times a month and every month.

You need to find out where your credit and your credit scores are in order to see where you qualify. That's the first place to start. Please ask the lender you are working with, "If my scores or credit does not meet the guidelines, can you help me or refer me to someone who can improve my credit and scores?"

Usually the banks and various lenders will not help you. I receive a lot of those turn downs from those banks where the clients tell me that they were told "you don't qualify", so goodbye. I could never figure out why when we are in a service industry to not discriminate against anyone who wants to acquire a home loan. I have coached many clients, six months, a year, two years and one client who took three years before he was able to purchase his home!

The best credit-repair companies are the ones that are licensed under the Department of Justice (DOJ). Please ensure before you pay any amount of money to ask if the lender is licensed under the DOJ. If they are not approved, move on. No matter what they say their track record is.

The only way that people maintain high FICO scores is derived from "equity in credit". What does this mean? In simple terms, if you have a credit card that has a $1,000.00 limit and you have a zero balance, then you have 100% in equity.

I have seen scores improve when someone had at least four credit cards. They keep them at zero balance for four months, their scores had improved over 100 points! If you maintain your credit card balances to 30% of the limit, you will also see an increase in your scores, as well. There is no secret to credit scores. As you can see, equity in credit makes all the difference in the world to help increase your scores.

What if you do not have credit? Then I would recommend building your credit. If banks or credit-card companies are not willing to provide a credit card, then the next best thing is to acquire secured credit cards. They work the same way. Only you need to open an account with the credit union, bank or other Visa card company. I have seen my clients open a secured credit card anywhere from $300.00 to $500.00. Opening a secured credit card just means you will provide those funds, $300.00 to $500 into a bank or credit union account where your funds are held as security for the credit card they provide.

The credit card will be reported to the credit bureaus to help your credit score increase. I have been told from past clients that the bank or credit union will usually give back the amount you've provided for security after a year has elapsed with on-time payments. So, if you are considering this option, be sure to ask if the bank or credit union will do this after a year. How far back do credit scores count credit? I have seen scores improve after four years have passed on charge offs, late payments or collections; the scores seem to improve along with the equity in credit. The key here is **"equity in credit". You need to build on that!**

If you want to see your true credit score, I recommend going to www.myfico.com. You will pay a small fee of $30-50 dollars for it, but it's definitely worth doing. Remember to request a MORTGAGE SCORE. This will let you know where you stand.

What if you do not want a lender to check your credit? You will never know where you stand! I have always recommended to clients to have their credit pulled. You need to start somewhere. Just jump!

Remember, the higher the FICO score the better the rate and program

Your success just doesn't happen to you.

Success happens because of what you do.

Income-Qualifying

If you are a W2 wage earner, Gross income is what will be used. Not your take-home pay. For the self-employed, the guidelines dictate to use a two-year average of the net income, NOT, your gross income. As of the date of this writing, guidelines have changed for the automated underwriting system. We have had several self-employed clients needing only to provide the current year of federal tax returns! That's right, only one year! I have seen this occur with someone that has high FICO scores, excellent credit, low ratios and longer than five years being self-employed.

If a self-employed borrower uses a schedule "C", the self-employed borrower is also allowed to add back the depreciation on that form to help qualify. This would include whatever your accountant has entered on the schedule "C" from equipment to vehicles you've purchased for business use. A corporation owner usually pays themselves with a pay stub and W2 along with the K1 income from the corporation. I must caution you here. Due to recent changes, you must show a distribution on the K1's. I have seen this done on Item 16 of that page and states "distribution" along with the amount listed.

Overtime income to be used must be with the same employer for two years. This is a strict guideline.

I had a client who worked for UPS part-time for one year. The next year, he was promoted to full-time. He made a huge amount of overtime, but in less than one year. He could have purchased a huge, higher-priced home using that overtime. We could only use his regular pay because of the guidelines. He did purchase a home that he qualified for. He now has a huge amount of equity in his home. After the two years passed, he had a bigger down payment from the sale of his home to acquire the home of his dreams.

The majority of clients who want to purchase a higher- priced home have waited the full two years or more. They come back, and then purchase the home of their dreams. You will never save as much money as from the equity you receive from owning a home. It does not matter the price of the home, it will gain appreciation. As of this writing, the FEDs have stated that we will see a 4.5% to 6.6% appreciation in equity for the next five years. **Time to jump off the fence!**

We also can qualify a person or persons who are seasonal workers. What are seasonal workers? Anyone who works so many months out of the year along with the ability to collect unemployment. There must be a two-year history of both. Your employer will be required to complete a verification of employment form that states this. We will use both incomes, unemployment and seasonal to get you qualified.

Social Security and retired recipients also qualify for home loans! Be prepared to provide your 1099's and award letters. Retirement income should provide a copy of the Social-Security distribution letter and also the W2's or 1099's depending on if they take out taxes or not.

The guidelines dictate a two-year history of employment verification. Unless the automated DU (Desktop Underwriter) system from

Fannie Mae or Freddie Mac states they require only one year of verification. I have had several clients who have received this type of automated approval. Some of these clients only needed to provide a current paystub and W2 from the previous year.

A true direct lender will only require the results from this report. I want to caution you that some lenders may have what we call "overlays". This means they will add on additional, more stringent, requirements-additional proof or documentation to substantiate your approval. These are very conservative lenders who want the cream of the crop for clients. You may ask the question, "Do you only go off the results from the automated DU approval or do you have add-ons?" Nine times out of ten, they will know. You need to be with a lender who only goes off the automated DU approval and those findings.

Due to the mortgage meltdown crisis that occurred in the late 2,000's, there has been many changes in qualifying for income requirements. If you have rental properties you derive income from, we will use a two-year average. This is the two years of your schedule "E" of your Federal Tax Returns only. If you are vacating your current residence to rent it out and purchase another personal residence, we can use the rental income from that property providing an appraisal is completed with a rental survey and operating income statement (this ensures that the rent is not inflated per guidelines). The appraisal for these types of loans usually run between $625-850 for future investment properties.

The majority of the loan programs, with the exception of the first-time home buyers' programs, will allow a non-occupant co-borrower to help qualify.

The ratios are what will determine the qualification of the monthly payment of the home loan. With the FHA program, the majority of lenders can go up to a back-end ratio of 55%. On conventional the max is 50%.

Ratios are derived from adding your payments on your credit debt and the actual house payment (principle, interest, taxes and insurance) and then dividing it by your gross income (before taxes), which will equal your back-end ratio. YES, it's that simple. **As explained above 50% or 55% example, new house pmt $2,000.00 plus credit debt and car payment of $1,200.00. total the two equals $3,200.00 divide that by your gross monthly income. Let's say it's $8,0000.00 equals 40% back end ratio.**

You should ready yourself to provide the following documents upfront in order for any lender to submit your loan to the underwriter for an actual underwritten disposition:

1. Two years FEDERAL TAX RETURNS, all pages
2. Federal returns only (no state taxes required)
3. Two years W2's and/or 1099's, if any
4. Award letters from retirement and social security income.
5. One full month current pay stubs
6. Two months current bank statements, all pages, all accounts including 401Ks, IRAs, and stocks, if any
7. Color copy of driver's licenses
8. Color copy of Social Security cards
9. If you own a current residence or rental property, the current month house-payment coupon including the home owner's insurance and property tax bill.
10. If you own a corporation receiving K1 income and own more than 26% of the corporation, you will need to provide the 1120 corp. returns as well, plus a profit and loss statement

year to date.

Providing this documentation upfront always helps speed up submitting your file to the underwriter. Recently, we have seen many clients receive an automated approval where the actual findings only required a current pay stub and verification of employment. Why? Because in these cases, the borrowers usually had high FICO scores, low credit balances with low payments, and a good down payment.

Rest assured, with an actual underwriter disposition, you can check the box on your purchase agreement to eliminate your loan contingency. The only contingency would be the appraisal and your property inspection.

By getting underwritten prior to going into contract, it will also speed up the time for closing. I have personally closed loans averaging 10-14 days. I actually had the record, one time, for closing a loan in four working days!! All because we had a buyer who was serious and cooperated with bringing everything upfront and paid for a rush on the appraisal! The seller, seller's agent, and buyer's agent all coordinated the fast close. It was a team effort from all involved.

Your offer will be accepted above others who only have a "pre-qual" when you are formally approved. How fast do you want to purchase a home and move in? That is entirely up to you. Get your documents in order TODAY!

The difference between those who want to be homeowners and those who actually achieve home ownership lies in your mindset and action

Assets

"Assets" is the one word that covers all the funds you have available in your checking accounts, savings accounts, CD accounts, 401Ks, IRAs and stocks and they need to be verified. The more of these accounts you have, the better the automated system will likely approve you. Reserves account for majority of approvals for those that are at the maximum limit of your purchasing power!

This section is pretty straight forward.

Due to the anti-money laundering act, we must verify any deposit into your account over $200.00 unless it is a business account. There is no way to get around this guideline.

Cash deposits cannot be verified. The underwriter will subtract those deposits from your funds. If you do not have enough leftover funds to cover the down payment and closing costs, you may have to acquire a gift from a family member. We have had this occur several times when we have taken over loans turned down from other banks and lenders.

If you are starting the process to see if you qualify for a home loan, ensure you are showing proof of any deposits over the amount of $200.00 into your personal bank account.

Prepare to ensure a two-month (60-day), clean history of your bank account. Do not move funds from one account to another. Keep your statements clean if you are thinking of purchasing a home.

We can use PayPal statements if you have a business or are a seller through various outlets.

As of this writing, we have had a numerous of clients who are now withdrawing funds out of their 401K and retirement accounts to purchase homes. We have parents helping with a gift for the down payments for their children to own a home. Gifts are always acceptable. If you are a donor, you must provide a current-month bank statement from any account that funds that will be provided from. You and the recipient will need to complete and sign a "Gift Letter Form" that your lender will provide. We always recommend wiring the funds directly from your account to the escrow company once your offer is accepted.

You are required to have seasoned funds, sixty days or more, sitting in your account. If you have sold an automobile, the guidelines will dictate you must provide a copy of your title, bill of sale, a Kelly Blue Book printout on its estimated value, and a copy of the check and deposit receipt going into your account. NO CASH!

Document, Document, Document. The government wants to ensure you are not participating in any type of money laundering or some other form of fraud to manipulate the system. We cannot use cash as any part of the purchase of your home. Always document your deposits and receipts. If you do not utilize direct deposit on your pay stubs, then we must see a deposit of the whole check. For example, if the check you receive from your employer is for $2,375.16 we must see a deposit for $2,375.16. if you want any cash back, do that in a separate transaction. This helps keep it clear and precise for the underwriter.

If you own a joint account with someone else that is not going on the loan, you will need a specific letter showing the name of the bank, the account number, stating from the other joint holder, and that you have 100% access and use of those funds in that account. Be ready to provide all asset documentation!

As of this writing, the seller is paying some sort of closing costs for our buyers in 99% of all my transactions. This is also important to know. Why? Because this helps with the amount of funds you will need to provide towards the purchase of your new home; this also is an asset in your favor.

The majority of the agents representing buyers will request that the seller pay 3% of the purchase price to help offset the buyers' closing costs. How do they do that. They ask.

But it depends on the seller. How long has the property been on the market? If the property has been on the market for a long time, a seller may consider paying a buyer's closing costs as opposed to reducing the price. Remember, everything is negotiable. The only thing a seller can say is "NO", right? I have had many thousands of sellers pay for our buyer's closing costs throughout my career. Many of those buyers have only had to provide their down payment. Sometimes, that may be the only funds you have available, besides a gift from a family member. Always ask the seller to help with your closing costs. Also if you are a seller and your property has not sold, this could be a good way of getting more buyers to look at your home.

Remember, do not move funds from one account to another. Do not show cash deposits. And, keep your statements clean sixty days prior to wanting to purchase your new home!

Are you just going to accept your life the way it is?

Or, are you going to lead your life?

If you take a look at successful people, they all lead their lives.

Collateral

Location, Location, Location! This has always been the most important part of the purchase process in the past and it will continue to be in the future! This is where value can make or break a deal.

In today's market, there are several factors that are combined to ensure the value of the property you are purchasing is proper for the collateral of your loan amount, besides Location, Location, Location, it could be Location, Quality and Amenities that help with the value of a home.

In the State of California, a home is required to have smoke alarms in every bedroom, a CO_2 detector in the hallway, and if it is a two-story home, CO_2 detectors are required for each floor. Also required are hot water heater straps, two straps. Check your state for specifications or your local professional real-estate agent.

I am always amazed on the appraisals that are completed that do not have a smoke alarm in one of the bedrooms or a CO_2 detector! You must always ensure that these items are in the home. If not, then you will be responsible to pay an additional $125.00 to $150.00 for reinspection. Ouch! Remember to ask your agent if they have been installed and, if not, to make sure that they are, or to write it into your contract and request that they be installed. If they are not installed at the time of inspection, the seller is responsible for the reinspection fee.

A true listing-agent professional will always have a termite report with a clearance and an inspection report with work required completed. Homes listed that have these are the ones you really want to look at because there is nothing that will come back to bite you later.

Is it better to have these upfront? Of course! Even if you must pay for these inspections yourself. A home inspection is worth its weight in gold! Remember, you and I see what's on the outside of the walls, while the inspectors see what's on the inside. They will check for water pressure, faulty electrical outlets or switches, anything that would create a health and safety issue. These inspections usually cost anywhere from $150.00 to $500.00. It really depends on the quality of the inspection. Again, your real-estate professional will have their "A" team of inspectors and contractors to help.

An appraiser will require any health and safety issues pertaining to the property as well. There have been cosmetics issues that an inspection report called out that the appraiser missed. Remember, it has to do with the habitability of the property for health and safety issues.

The appraiser is required to take pictures of the hot water heater, stove with the gas on, and a faucet showing running water. If there are stains in the ceiling, the appraiser will call for a roof certification. Exposed wood will need to be painted, especially peeling paint, which will be required to be scraped and repainted. Any blatant dry rot must be repaired and completed per the guidelines. With blatant dry rot, the appraiser may call for a termite report and clearance. What happens if your appraisal comes in at a lower value than your sales price? Seldom have I had this occur throughout my years in this industry. When it does, there are two options:

1. The first option is for the seller to accept the new value-the value established that you are purchasing came from somewhere. It is usually the listing agent's responsibility to provide the comparables (similar homes that have sold and closed within the home's vicinity) to the appraiser when he arrives at the property. If the listing agent did not show up then that is on them. This is my opinion.

What happens if the seller is not willing to reduce his price? Then it's up to your agent to represent you in negotiating new terms/sales price. Ultimately, you have the option of walking away.

2. The second option is to request a "reconsideration of value". Then the listing agent would provide justification for a higher value. The appraiser is provided additional homes from the listing agent to justify why they listed the home at the current value, especially if there are other back-up offers and remember, one of them could be cash, which could be more attractive to the seller. There have been many transactions where clients have purchased above the appraised value.

The appraisal is then thoroughly reviewed by the underwriter who may request additional items to complete the deal. I had one instance where they requested an additional comparable. Since there were no more recent comparables available, the appraiser had to go back six months on homes sold. The appraiser found a similar property that helped with the value.

Always consult with your realtor on any concerns you have with the property. **Remember, you are the one who is going to live in this home! No one else!**

"If you can dream it, you can achieve it."

– ZIG ZIGLAR

Clear To Close! Who-Hoo!

These are the best words to hear in any transaction! Once the appraisal has been reviewed and signed off by the underwriter, along with any other nickel and dime conditions, we have a CLEAR TO CLOSE!

This means you have been completely signed off to close the loan. A Closing Disclosure, CD, for short will then be issued. You will be required to sign and date this form. This form provides the exact amount of the down payment and closing costs for you to provide to the escrow company. Everything that has been explained to you about your total investment from your lender is in this CD.

This form was created by the FEDS under what we call TRID. What you need to know is that once you sign this form, we all must wait three days before we can make an appointment to have you sign your loan documents. Three days is the waiting period. There is no deviation on a purchase or refinance. This time allows a buyer to make a decision if something is not right with the interest rate, fees, or down payment. You have a right to contest your figures.

During this waiting period is the best time for you to wire your funds to the escrow company. You will be required to provide a copy of the wire receipt from your bank along with a history printout showing the funds came from your account. This is the account your down payment and closing costs were verified to come from. There are lenders who will have you sign in the morning and fund your loan to have it recorded the same day. A good question to ask your loan officer is, "Will our funding and recording of our loan happen on the same day when we sign? If not, when"? "Next day or two days later"? This is a very good question to ask!

Remember, throughout your transaction, there is no such thing as a DUMB question. You do not do this on a daily basis as your Loan officer does. So, ask any questions you have concerns about!

So, what is next after you sign your loan documents? We wait for the escrow-title company to have your loan recorded once your loan is funded by your lender.

The role of the escrow company is that it is a third, non-interested party that gathers and abides by all of your contracts, addendums and counter offers. It will collect an earnest money deposit, per your contract once your offer is accepted. It will receive and review the preliminary title report from the title company for your review. Based on the preliminary title report, it will also request a demand pay off from the seller's lender and any other liens or collections listed on the report. They will disperse funds at the close of escrow to any entity that is owed any funds. They also will provide you with a closing statement and usually a small refund to you if any is owed.

You will need to save the closing statement for the end of the year to provide your tax accountant… remember to create a file of your home documents. You will receive a copy of ALL your loan documents you have signed.

Congratulations! You are now a new home owner!

You have achieved the American Dream of Home Ownership!

Who-hoo!

Ed Fontes has been involved in several facets of the real-estate industry for over 39 years from construction, new homes, and real estate to eventually finance and lending, from land to commercial properties, to eventually home loans as a top producer. The majority of those years, Ed has been a branch manager with a variety of local and super-regional organizations.

His wealth of knowledge and expertise has helped many thousands of clients achieve the American Dream of Home Ownership.

**If you are interested in obtaining a home loan,
you can contact Ed at:
Cell: 916-712-8509 Fax: 844-303-3434
NMLS#233325
emails: edfontes@edfontes.com – efontes@amerifirst.us**

Ed can also be found on the following social-media sites:

www.edfontes.com
https://www.youtube.com/channel/UCYTFqFZw3qjDK7IqeJeOG-Q
https://plus.google.com/106793557448066542302/posts?hl=en
https://www.facebook.com/edfontes0
https://www.linkedin.com/in/edfontes
http://activerain.trulia.com/profile/edfontes
https://www.pinterest.com/edfontes/

www.ingramcontent.com/pod-product-compliance
Lightning Source LLC
Chambersburg PA
CBHW072245170526
45158CB00003BA/1009